Librarians help people find books.

Read for a Better World™

LIBRARIANS

A First Look

PERCY LEED

GRL Consultant, Diane Craig, Certified Literacy Specialist

Lerner Publications ◆ Minneapolis

Educator Toolbox

Reading books is a great way for kids to express what they're interested in. Before reading this title, ask the reader these questions:

What do you think this book is about? Look at the cover for clues.

What do you already know about librarians?

What do you want to learn about librarians?

Let's Read Together

Encourage the reader to use the pictures to understand the text.

Point out when the reader successfully sounds out a word.

Praise the reader for recognizing sight words such as *in* and *a*.

TABLE OF CONTENTS

Librarians

Librarians work in a library.
They help people learn.

They help people use computers too.

Students may need to learn something for school. Librarians help them.

What is the library like at your school?

Librarians put books away when people are done reading them.

Some librarians read to kids. They have story time.

Have you ever been to story time?

Some librarians plan things for kids to do. They may run a book club.

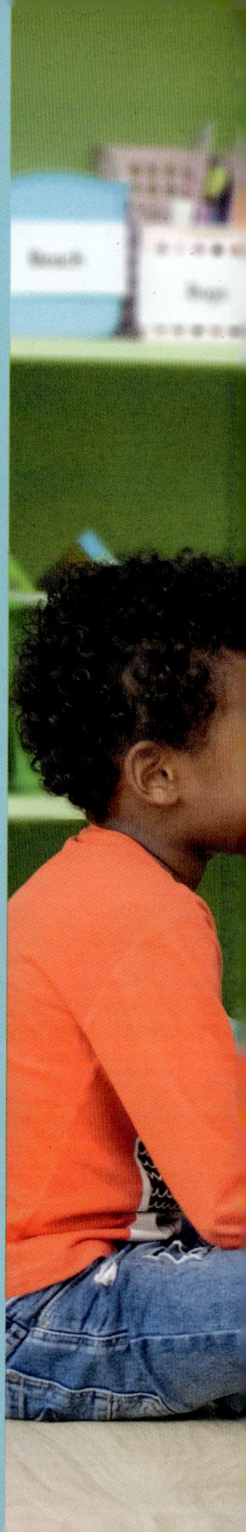

A library may have a space to play.

Librarians help keep this space clean and safe.

Librarians go to school for many years.

Why must librarians go to school?

Librarians work hard.
They help us learn!

You Connect!

What is something you like about librarians?

How can a librarian help you?

Would you like to be a librarian when you grow up?

Social and Emotional Snapshot

Student voice is crucial to building reader confidence. Ask the reader:

What is your favorite part of this book?

What is something you learned from this book?

Did this book remind you of any community helpers you've met?

Photo Glossary

club

computers

library

story time

Learn More

Bassier, Emma. *Libraries*. Minneapolis: Pop!, 2020.

Kaiser, Brianna. *All about Librarians*. Minneapolis: Lerner Publications, 2023.

Tornito, Maria. *A Day with a Librarian*. Minneapolis: Jump!, 2022.

Index

Photo Acknowledgments

The images in this book are used with the permission of: © wavebreakmedia/Shutterstock Images, pp. 4–5, 6, 8–9, 23 (bottom left); © SDI Productions/iStockphoto, pp. 7, 12–13, 23 (top right, bottom right); © Trish233/iStockphoto, pp. 10–11; © weedezign/Adobe Stock, pp. 14–15, 23 (top left); © FatCamera/iStockphoto, p. 16; © Hispanolistic/iStockphoto, p. 17; © PeopleImages/iStockphoto, pp. 18–19; © kali9/iStockphoto, p. 20.

Cover Photograph: © Wavebreakmedia/iStockphoto

Design Elements: © Mighty Media, Inc.

Lerner Publications Company
An imprint of Lerner Publishing Group, Inc.
241 First Avenue North
Minneapolis, MN 55401 USA

For reading levels and more information, look up this title at www.lernerbooks.com.

Main body text set in Mikado a Medium.
Typeface provided by Hannes von Doehren.

Library of Congress Cataloging-in-Publication Data

Names: Leed, Percy, 1968–author.
Title: Librarians : a first look / Percy Leed.
Description: Minneapolis, Minneapolis : Lerner Publications, 2024. | Series: Read about community helpers | Includes bibliographical references and index. | Audience: Ages 5–8. | Audience: Grades K–1. | Summary: "Sometimes it can be hard to find books that interest us. With the help of a librarian, reading can be fun. This book helps readers better understand why librarians are the real MVPs at school"— Provided by publisher.
Identifiers: LCCN 2023035574 (print) | LCCN 2023035575 (ebook) | ISBN 9798765626436 (library binding) | ISBN 9798765629550 (paperback) | ISBN 9798765636886 (epub)
Subjects: LCSH: Librarians—Juvenile literature.
Classification: LCC Z682 .L397 2024 (print) | LCC Z682 (ebook) | DDC 027.8/222—dc23/eng/20231025

LC record available at https://lccn.loc.gov/2023035574
LC ebook record available at https://lccn.loc.gov/2023035575

Manufactured in the United States of America
1 - CG - 7/15/24